Especially for

_____

From

_____

Date

_____

© 2009 by Barbour Publishing, Inc.

ISBN 978-1-61626-415-4

Several text selections were compiled from the following: *In Celebration of a New Day*, *365 Days of Purpose for Women*, *365 Days of Wisdom for Busy Women*, *365 Days of Hope*, *365 Prayers for Women*, *365 Encouraging Words for Women*, *365 Inspirational Quotes*, *365 Favorite Quotes for Dads*, *365 Favorite Quotes for Grandmothers*, *365 Favorite Quotes for Friends*, *365 Inspiring Moments for Teachers*, *365 Moments of Peace for Moms* published by Barbour Publishing, Inc.

Published by Barbour Publishing, Inc., P.O. Box 719, Uhrichsville, Ohio 44683, www.barbourbooks.com

Our mission is to publish and distribute inspirational products offering exceptional value and biblical encouragement to the masses.

Member of the
Evangelical Christian
Publishers Association

Printed in China.

Whispers of Encouragement

DAILY INSPIRATION FOR WOMEN

BARBOUR
PUBLISHING

Embrace Today

Embrace the wonder and
excitement each day brings.
For tomorrow affords us new
opportunities. . .time to
experience. . .time to create. . .
time to reflect. . .time to dream.

UNKNOWN

Look Forward

Tomorrow is a new day; you shall
begin it serenely and with too high
a spirit to be encumbered with your
old nonsense. This day is all that is
good and fair. It is too dear, with its
hopes and invitations, to waste
a moment on yesterdays.

RALPH WALDO EMERSON

You Are Not Alone

Father, when troubles come, I never have to face them alone. Thank You for always being with me as my refuge and strength. When all else fails, I put my trust in You and am never disappointed. Amen.

God's Love Is Everywhere

What inexpressible joy for me,
to look up through the apple
blossoms and the fluttering leaves,
and to see God's love there. . .
to look beyond to the bright blue
depths of the sky, and feel they are
a canopy of blessing—the roof of
the house of my Father.

ELIZABETH RUNDELL CHARLES

Beautiful Virtue

Beauty is the mark God sets on virtue. Every natural action is graceful; every heroic act is also decent, and causes the place and the bystanders to shine.

RALPH WALDO EMERSON

Today Is a Gift

This bright, new day, complete with
24 hours of opportunities, choices,
and attitudes comes with a perfectly
matched set of 1,440 minutes.
This unique gift, this one day, cannot
be exchanged, replaced, or refunded.
Handle with care. Make the most of it.

Unknown

Mustard Seed Faith

*"If you have faith as small as
a mustard seed, you can say to this
mountain, 'Move from here to there'
and it will move. Nothing will
be impossible for you."*

MATTHEW 17:20—21 NIV

Acts of Caring

Too often we underestimate the power of a touch, a smile, a kind word, a listening ear, an honest compliment, or the smallest acts of caring, all of which have the potential to turn a life around.

LEO BUSCAGLIA

Our Only Response

We are of such value to God that He came to live among us. . .and to guide us home. He will go to any length to seek us, even to being lifted high upon the cross to draw us back to Himself. We can only respond by loving God for His love.

CATHERINE OF SIENA

Daily Joys

Daily duties are daily joys,
because they are something
which God gives us to offer unto
Him, to do our very best,
in acknowledgement of His love.

EDWARD BOUVERIE PUSEY

The Sun Still Shines

Even in winter, even in the midst
of the storm, the sun is still there.
Somewhere, up above the clouds,
it still shines and warms and pulls
at the life buried deep inside the
brown branches and frozen earth.
The sun is there! Spring will come!
The clouds cannot stay forever!

GLORIA GAITHER

Live the Life You Imagined

If one advances confidently in the direction of his dreams and endeavors to live the life which he has imagined, he will meet with success unexpected in common hours. Go confidently in the direction of your dreams! Live the life you've imagined!

HENRY DAVID THOREAU

What We Need

What we need is not new light, but new sight; not new paths, but new strength to walk in the old ones; not new duties but new wisdom from on high to fulfill those that are plain before us.

UNKNOWN

Run with Perseverance

Let us run with perseverance the race marked out for us. Let us fix our eyes on Jesus, the author and perfecter of our faith, who for the joy set before him endured the cross, scorning its shame, and sat down at the right hand of the throne of God.

HEBREWS 12:1–2 NIV

Voyage of Discovery

We are all inventors, each sailing out on a voyage of discovery, guided each by a private chart, of which there is no duplicate. The world is all gates, all opportunities.

RALPH WALDO EMERSON

Surrendered to God

It is wonderful what miracles God works in wills that are utterly surrendered to Him. He turns hard things into easy, and bitter things into sweet. It is not that He puts easy things in the place of the hard, but he actually changes the hard thing into the easy one.

HANNAH WHITALL SMITH

My Anchor Holds

And it holds, my anchor holds;
Blow your wildest then, O gale,
On my bark so small and frail,
By His grace I shall not fail,
For my anchor holds,
My anchor holds.

W. C. MARTIN

Strong Faith

As your faith is strengthened,
you will find that there is no longer
the need to have a sense of control,
that things will flow as they will,
and that you will flow with them,
to your great delight and benefit.

Emmanuel Teney

Reason for the Journey

We may run, walk, stumble, drive,
or fly, but let us never lose sight of
the reason for the journey or miss a
chance to see a rainbow on the way.

GLORIA GAITHER

He Has Prepared a Way

*"For I know the plans I have for you,"
declares the LORD, "plans to prosper you
and not to harm you, plans to give you
hope and a future. Then you will call
upon me and come and pray to me,
and I will listen to you."*

JEREMIAH 29:11–12 NIV

He Will Care for You

Father, help me realize that my wants are temporary and of little importance. Let me lean against You, Lord, relaxed in the knowledge that You will care for me. Amen.

Today Is Your Best Day

As God's child, today is your best day
because you are totally and completely
dependent upon Him. . . . God is your
only rock, your only security, your only
certainty, and your only hope.

ROY LESSIN

God Is There Already

God is down in front. He is in
the tomorrows. It is tomorrow that
fills [us] with dread. God is there
already. All the tomorrows of our
life have to pass Him before
they can get to us.

F. B. MEYER

Abide with God

I long for scenes where
man has never trod;
A place where woman
never smil'd or wept;
There to abide with my creator, God,
And sleep as I in
childhood sweetly slept;
Untroubling and untroubled
where I lie;
The grass below—
above the vaulted sky.

JOHN CLARE

I Will Do

I am only one, but I am one.
I cannot do everything,
but I can do something.
And that which I can do,
by the grace of God, I will do.

DWIGHT L. MOODY

Here I Am

Here I am, Lord—body, heart,
and soul. Grant that with Your love,
I may be big enough to reach
the world, and small enough to
be at one with You.

MOTHER TERESA

Uncut Diamonds

Guard well your spare moments.
They are like uncut diamonds.
Discard them and their value
will never be known. Improve
them and they will become the
brightest gems in a useful life.

RALPH WALDO EMERSON

God Calls You to Hope

I pray also that the eyes of your heart
may be enlightened in order that
you may know the hope to which
he has called you, the riches of his
glorious inheritance in the saints,
and his incomparably great power
for us who believe.

EPHESIANS 1:18–19 NIV

React with Praise

Whenever you react with praise and thanksgiving for an opportunity to grow more like Jesus in your way of reacting to things, instead of grumbling or feeling self-pity, you will find that the whole situation will be changed into a great blessing.

Hannah Hurnard

Beauty of His Peace

Drop Thy still dews of quietness,
Till all our strivings cease;
Take from our souls the
strain and stress,
And let our ordered lives confess
The beauty of Thy peace.

JOHN GREENLEAF WHITTIER

The Tide Will Turn

When you get into a tight place and everything goes against you, till it seems as though you could not hang on a minute longer, never give up then, for that is just the place and time that the tide will turn.

HARRIET BEECHER STOWE

Present Blessings

Reflect upon your present blessings
of which every man has many;
not on your past misfortunes of
which all men have some.

CHARLES DICKENS

Hold to His Teaching

To the Jews who had believed him, Jesus said, "If you hold to my teaching, you are really my disciples. Then you will know the truth, and the truth will set you free."

JOHN 8:31–32 NIV

Rewarding Joy

The marvelous richness of human
experience would lose something
of rewarding joy if there were no
limitations to overcome.
The hilltop hour would not be
half so wonderful if there were no
dark valleys to traverse.

HELEN KELLER

You Are Indispensable

Everyone has a unique role to
fill in the world and is important
in some respect. Everyone,
including and perhaps especially
you, is indispensable.

NATHANIEL HAWTHORNE

Faith Illuminates the Way

Dark as my path may seem to others, I carry a magic light in my heart. Faith, the spiritual strong searchlight, illumines the way, and although sinister doubts lurk in the shadow, I walk unafraid toward the enchanted wood where the foliage is always green, where joy abides. . .in the presence of the Lord.

HELEN KELLER

Gratitude

Lord, thank You for every
blessing, both big and small.
Help me to be more aware of
the ways in which You take care
of me, so my gratitude can
continue to grow. Amen.

God Restores

[God]. . .rekindles burned-out lives
with fresh hope, restoring dignity
and respect to their lives—a place
in the sun! For the very structures of
earth are GOD's; he has laid out his
operations on a firm foundation.

1 SAMUEL 2:8—9 MSG

Look Fear in the Face

You gain strength, courage, and confidence by every experience in which you really stop to look fear in the face. You must do the thing that you think you cannot do.

ELEANOR ROOSEVELT

Faith with Freedom

So long as faith
with freedom reigns,
And loyal hope survives,
And gracious charity remains
To leaven lowly lives;
While there is one untrodden tract
For intellect or will,
And men are free to think and act,
Life is worth living still.

ALFRED AUSTIN

Ask for Grace

Grace is available for each of us every day. . .but we've got to remember to ask for it with a grateful heart and not worry about whether there will be enough for tomorrow.

SARAH BAN BREATHNACH

The Gift of Making Friends

Blessed are they who have the gift of making friends, for it is one of God's best gifts. It involves many things, but above all the power of going out of one's self and appreciating what is noble and loving in another.

THOMAS HUGHES

Be Available for God's Work

You simply have to be yourself—
at any age—as God made you,
available to Him so that He can
work in and through you to bring
about His kingdom and His glory.

LUCI SWINDOLL

Step out in Service

Your heart is beating with God's
love; open it to others. He has
entrusted you with gifts and talents;
use them for His service. He goes
before you each step of the way;
walk in faith. Take courage.
Step out into the unknown with
the One who knows all.

ELLYN SANNA

Forever

Forever, Lord—what encouragement is in that word. We have all eternity to spend with You in heaven. Thank You for this indescribable gift. Thank You for being the Alpha and the Omega, the first and the last. Amen.

The World of the Generous

The world of the generous gets larger and larger. . . . The one who blesses others is abundantly blessed; those who help others are helped.

PROVERBS 11:24–25 MSG

My Crown

My crown is in my heart,
not on my head,
Not decked with diamonds
and Indian stones,
Nor to be seen;
my crown is called content;
A crown it is that seldom
kings enjoy.

WILLIAM SHAKESPEARE, *HENRY VI*

Success in Life

If you wish success in life, make
perseverance your bosom friend,
experience your wise counselor,
caution your elder brother,
and hope your guardian genius.

JOSEPH ADDISON

Go Above and Beyond

Excellence can be attained if
you care more than others think
is wise, risk more than others
think is safe, dream more than
others think is practical,
and expect more than others
think is possible.

UNKNOWN

Make Others Happy

Try to make at least one person
happy every day, and then in ten
years you may have made 3,650
persons happy, or brightened a
small town by your contribution to
the fund of general enjoyment.

SYDNEY SMITH

Love and Friendship

Human love and the delights
of friendship, out of which are
built the memories that endure,
are also to be treasured up as hints
of what shall be hereafter.

BEDE JARRETT

Those Who Wait upon God

For even young people tire and drop out, young folk in their prime stumble and fall. But those who wait upon God get fresh strength. They spread their wings and soar like eagles. They run and don't get tired, they walk and don't lag behind.

ISAIAH 40:30–31 MSG

The Strength of Cheerfulness

Wondrous is the strength of cheerfulness, and its power of endurance—the cheerful man will do more in the same time, will do it better, will preserve it longer, than the sad or sullen.

THOMAS CARLYLE

What Waits over the Horizon

The best thing we can hope for in this life is a knothole peek at the shining realities ahead. Yet a glimpse is enough. It's enough to convince our hearts that whatever sufferings and sorrows currently assail us aren't worthy of comparison to that which waits over the horizon.

JONI EARECKSON TADA

Joy

Joy is prayer. Joy is strength.
Joy is love. Joy is a net of love
by which you can catch souls.
She gives most who gives with joy.

MOTHER TERESA

Carve Your Name On Hearts

A good character is the best tombstone. Those who loved you, and were helped by you, will remember you when the forget-me-nots are withered. Carve your name on hearts, and not on marble.

CHARLES H. SPURGEON

The Happiness of Life

The happiness of life is made up of minute fractions—the little, soon-forgotten charities of a kiss or a smile, a kind look or a heartfelt compliment.

SAMUEL TAYLOR COLERIDGE

Love Unselfishly

Instead of being unhappy, just let
your love grow as God wants it to
grow. Seek goodness in others.
Love more persons more. . .
unselfishly, without thought of
return. The return, never fear,
will take care of itself.

HENRY DRUMMOND

Instead of Worrying, Pray

Don't fret or worry. Instead of worrying, pray. Let petitions and praises shape your worries into prayers, letting God know your concerns. Before you know it, a sense of God's wholeness, everything coming together for good, will come and settle you down.

PHILIPPIANS 4:6–7 MSG

The Father's Solace

Heavenly Father, I find it hard to find time to relax. Thank You for making me to lie down even when I don't want to. Thank You for leading me beside quiet waters when I need the solace. Amen.

Hope

Hope is not the conviction
that something will turn
out well, but the certainty that
something makes sense
regardless of how it turns out.

VÁCLAV HAVEL

Going God's Way

The strength and the happiness
of a man consists in finding out
the way in which God is going,
and going in that way, too.

HENRY WARD BEECHER

The Word of God

For the word of God is living and active. Sharper than any doubled-edged sword, it penetrates even to dividing soul and spirit, joints and marrow; it judges the thoughts and attitudes of the heart.

HEBREWS 4:12 NIV

God's Spirit Changes Us

God offers us His Spirit, not just as an encouragement, but as a heart-changer. He enters into us and begins to redesign our interior life. Suddenly our actions and our words are truthful, kind, and fair. No longer do they reflect the blackness that painted our hearts, but the rainbow of colors of His blessings.

Pamela McQuade

DAY 65

Be God's Kindness

Let no one ever come to you
without leaving better and
happier. Be the living expression
of God's kindness: kindness in
your face, kindness in your eyes,
kindness in your smile.

MOTHER TERESA

The Future Starts Now!

*What a God we have! And how
fortunate we are to have him,
this Father of our Master Jesus!
Because Jesus was raised from the dead,
we've been given a brand-new life
and have everything to live for,
including a future in heaven—
and the future starts now!*

1 Peter 1:3–4 msg

Be Glad of Life

Be glad of life, because it gives you
the chance to love and to work and to
play and to look up at the stars; to be
satisfied with your possessions. . .
to think seldom of your enemies,
often of your friends, and every day of
Christ; and to spend as much time as
you can, with body and with spirit in
God's out-of-doors—these are little
guideposts on the footpath to peace.

HENRY VAN DYKE

No Limit to His Blessings

His love has no limits,
His grace has no measure,
His power no boundary
known unto men;
For out of His infinite
riches in Jesus
He giveth, and giveth,
and giveth again.

ANNIE JOHNSON FLINT

Keep Happy and Joyful

Joy is the holy fire that keeps
our purpose warm and our
intelligence aglow. Work without
joy is nothing. Resolve to keep
happy, and your joy and you
shall form an invincible host
against difficulties.

HELEN KELLER

A Sacredness in Tears

There is a sacredness in tears.
They are not the mark of weakness,
but of power. They speak more
eloquently than ten thousand
tongues. They are the messengers
of overwhelming grief, of deep
contrition, and of unspeakable love.

WASHINGTON IRVING

How Beautiful to Be Alive

How beautiful it is to be alive!
To wake each morn as
if the Maker's grace
Did us afresh from
nothingness derive,
That we might sing
"How happy is our case!
How beautiful it is to be alive!"

HENRY SEPTIMUS SUTTON

I Am Your Child

Lord, I am Your child, and You
delight in me whenever I fall.
You pick me up, give me a hug,
and encourage me to try again.
Thank You for rejoicing over me.

RACHEL QUILLIN AND NANCY J. FARRIER

Hope

Hope floods my heart with
delight! Running on air,
mad with life, dizzy, reeling,
Upward I mount—
faith is sight, life is feeling,
Hope is the day-star of might!

MARGARET WITTER FULLER

The Days of Childhood

Let me play in the sunshine;
Let me sing for joy;
Let me grow in the light;
Let me splash in the rain,
And remember the days of
my childhood forever.

UNKNOWN

Wait for the Lord

*I wait for the LORD, my soul waits,
and in his word I put my hope.
My soul waits for the LORD more than
watchmen wait for the morning. . . .
For with the LORD is unfailing love
and with him is full redemption.*

PSALM 130:5–7 NIV

Keep Hearts Young and Eyes Open

Half the joy of life is in little things taken on the run. Let us run if we must. . .but let us keep our hearts young and our eyes open that nothing worth our while shall escape us. And everything is worth its while if we only grasp it and its significance.

CHARLES VICTOR CHERBULIEZ

No More Fear

Lord, remove the fears that bind me so that I can be happy in the knowledge that You are there to comfort me—no matter what else is happening. Amen.

An Upward Leap of the Heart

Prayer is an upward leap of the heart, an untroubled glance toward heaven, a cry of gratitude and love which I utter from the depths of sorrow as well as from the heights of joy. It has supernatural grandeur that expands the soul and unites it with God.

THÈRÉSE OF LISIEUX

Dust in the Balance

All the joy and delight, all the pleasures a thousand worlds could offer, are as dust in the balance when weighed against one hour of this mutual exchange of love and communion with the Lord.

CORA HARRIS MACILRAVY

Pay Praises for Blessings

The sun. . .in its full glory,
Either at rising or setting—this
And many other like
blessings we enjoy daily;
And for the most of them,
Because they are so common,
Most men forget to pay their praises.
But let not us.

IZAAK WALTON

Depend upon Him

Let us begin from this moment
to acknowledge Him in all our
ways, and do everything,
whatsoever we do, as service
to Him and for His glory,
depending upon Him alone for
wisdom, and strength,
and sweetness, and patience.

HANNAH WHITALL SMITH

DAY 82

Look forward with Hope

Do not look forward to the changes
and chances of this life in fear;
rather look to them with full hope
that, as they arise, God, whose you
are, will deliver you out of them.

ST. FRANCIS DE SALES

Courage Is from the Heart

The word *courage* comes from the Latin word for *heart*—and courage is born in the heart. Courageous acts come from the heart. And a courageous life is lived from the heart. So live your life from your heart, and you will find the courage you need entwined in your living.

UNKNOWN

Another Chance

If you have made mistakes,
even serious ones, there is always
another chance for you. What we
call failure is not the falling down,
but the staying down.

MARY PICKFORD

As Others See You

My friend, if I could give you one thing, I would wish for you the ability to see yourself as others see you. Then you would realize what a truly special person you are.

B. A. BILLINGSLY

Count Flowers

When we start to count flowers,
we cease to count weeds;
When we start to count blessings,
we cease to count needs;
When we start to count laughter,
we cease to count tears;
When we start to count memories,
we cease to count years.

UNKNOWN

Sailing to Eternity

The river of Thy grace
is flowing free;
We launch upon its
depths to sail to Thee.
In the ocean of Thy
love we soon shall be;
We are sailing to eternity.

PAUL RADER

Day 88

Eternal Encouragement

May our Lord Jesus Christ himself and God our Father, who loved us and by his grace gave us eternal encouragement and good hope, encourage your hearts and strengthen you in every good deed and word.

2 Thessalonians 2:16–17 NIV

God's Burden

A burden, even a small one,
when carried alone and in
isolation can destroy us,
but a burden when carried
as part of God's burden can
lead us to new life. That is the
great mystery of our faith.

HENRI NOUWEN

Trust God

Take hours, minutes, and moments
as they come, one at a time. Don't
run ahead. Do what you can now. . .
and at the end of the day, let it go.
Put all that is left undone in God's
hands. God is at work in ways you
cannot see. Trust Him. Sleep. . .
rest. . .relax in His arms.

ELLYN SANNA

The Simple Things

When we take time to notice the
simple things in life, we never lack
for encouragement. We discover we
are surrounded by limitless hope
that's just wearing everyday clothes.

UNKNOWN

The Father Guides

Father, I get discouraged when
I don't know which way to go.
Remind me that You are right
behind me, telling me which way
to turn. Help me to be quiet and
listen for your guidance. Amen.

Obey Jesus' Teaching

Jesus replied, "If anyone loves me,
he will obey my teaching.
My Father will love him,
and we will come to him and
make our home with him."

JOHN 14:23 NIV

Hope Doesn't Fail

When God holds us up, weariness need not destroy us. We can rest in God, then continue on with a firm step. Through prayer and scripture, refreshment comes, along with a new sense of purpose. Hope does not fail when it's put in the Savior.

PAMELA MCQUADE

Bound to Be True

I am not bound to win, but I am bound to be true. I am not bound to succeed, but I am bound to live by the light that I have. I must stand with anybody that stands right, stand with him while he is right, and part [company] with him when he goes wrong.

ABRAHAM LINCOLN

Unique Creation

The way you are put together is unique—different from any other. Even identical twins can be distinguished by voice or mannerisms. God has designed you wonderfully well. He thinks about you every minute of every day. He has a special purpose just for you, a niche that only you can fill.

LORI SHANKLE

Live Full Lives

*Live full lives, full in the fullness
of God. God can do anything,
you know—far more than you
could ever imagine or guess or
request in your wildest dreams!
He does it not by pushing us around
but by working within us, his Spirit
deeply and gently within us.*

EPHESIANS 3:19–20 MSG

A Bigger Picture

There is something satisfying,
rejuvenating, comforting about the
seasons. They remind me that I play
one small part in a much bigger
picture—that there is a pulse,
a sequence, a journey set into motion
by the very hand of God Himself.

KAREN SCALF LINAMEN

Where He Delights to Dwell

All God's glory and beauty come from within, and there He delights to dwell. His visits there are frequent, His conversation sweet, His comforts refreshing, His peace passing all understanding.

THOMAS á KEMPIS

Open Wide

Open wide the windows of our
spirits and fill us full of light;
open wide the door of our hearts,
that we may receive and entertain
Thee with all our powers of adoration.

CHRISTINA ROSSETTI

A Bright Torch

Life is no brief candle to me.
It is a sort of splendid torch which
I have got a hold of for the
moment, and I want to make
it burn as brightly as possible
before handing it on to future
generations.

GEORGE BERNARD SHAW

Kind Words

Kind words produce their
own image in men's souls;
and a beautiful image it is.
They soothe and quiet and
comfort the hearer. . . .
We have not yet begun to use
kind words in such abundance
as they ought to be used.

BLAISE PASCAL

The Good Shepherd

Father, Your guidance is
trustworthy. You are our Good
Shepherd. You lead us to places
of rest when we need them.
Thank You for Your leading. Amen.

God Gives Endurance and Encouragement

For everything that was written in the past was written to teach us, so that through endurance and the encouragement of the Scriptures we might have hope. May the God who gives endurance and encouragement give you a spirit of unity among yourselves.

ROMANS 15:4–5 NIV

Shining Through

As a countenance is
made beautiful by the soul's
shining through it, so the world
is beautiful by the shining
through it of God.

FRIEDRICH HEINRICH JACOBI

Nurture the Spirit of Stillness

Do whatever is necessary to nurture the spirit of stillness in your life. Don't let the enemy wear you so thin that you lose your balance and perspective. Regular time for stillness is as important and necessary as sleep, exercise, and nutritional food.

EMILIE BARNES

Appreciate the Beauty and Wonder

I find each day too short for all the
thoughts I want to think, all the
walks I want to take, all the books
I want to read, and all the friends
I want to see. The longer I live,
the more my mind dwells upon the
beauty and the wonder of the world.

JOHN BURROUGHS

As I Am

Grace means God accepts me just
as I am. He does not require or
insist that I measure up to someone
else's standard of performance.
He loves me completely, thoroughly,
and perfectly. There is nothing I can
do to add to or detract from that love.

MARY GRAHAM

The Lord Will Be Your Confidence

Have no fear of sudden disaster or of the ruin that overtakes the wicked, for the LORD will be your confidence and will keep your foot from being snared.

PROVERBS 3:25–26 NIV

Unutterable Fulfillment

Occasionally in my life there are those moments of unutterable fulfillment which cannot be completely explained by those symbols called words. Their meanings can only be articulated by the inaudible language of the heart.

MARTIN LUTHER KING JR.

Leave a Hopeful Impulse

Every heart that has beat strong and
cheerfully has left a hopeful impulse
behind it in the world and bettered
the tradition of mankind.

ROBERT LOUIS STEVENSON

Shine On Others

Dear Lord. . .shine through me,
and be so in me that every soul I
come in contact with may feel Your
presence in my soul. . . . Let me thus
praise You in the way You love best,
by shining on those around me.

JOHN HENRY NEWMAN

Discover the Good News!

Everyone has inside of him a piece of good news. The good news is that you don't know how great you can be! How much you can love! What you can accomplish! And what your potential is!

ANNE FRANK

A Still, Small Voice

There is a voice, "a still,
small voice" of love,
Heard from above;
But not amidst the
din of earthly sounds,
Which here confounds;
By those withdrawn
apart it best is heard,
And peace, sweet peace
Breathes in each gentle word.

UNKNOWN

A Thankful Spirit

Make it a rule to yourself to thank and praise God for everything that happens to you. For it is certain that whatever seeming calamity happens to you, if you thank and praise God for it, you turn it into a blessing.

WILLIAM LAW

Keep Moving in the Right Direction

I find the great thing in this world
is not so much where we stand,
as in what direction we are moving.
To reach the port of heaven, we must
sail sometimes with the wind and
sometimes against it—but we must
sail, and not drift, nor lie at anchor.

OLIVER WENDELL HOLMES

God Promises Life without End

*My aim is to raise hopes
by pointing the way to life
without end. This is the life
God promised long ago—
and he doesn't break promises!*

TITUS 1:2 MSG

God Is Everywhere

There's not a tint that paints the rose
Or decks the lily fair,
Or marks the humblest
flower that grows,
But God has placed it there. . . .
There's not a place on
earth's vast round,
In ocean's deep or air,
Where love and beauty are not found,
For God is everywhere.

UNKNOWN

Trust Him

Trust Him when dark
doubts assail thee.
Trust Him when thy
strength is small.
Trust Him when to simply trust Him
Seems the hardest thing of all.
Trust Him, He is ever faithful;
Trust Him, for He is the best;
Trust Him, for the heart of Jesus
Is the only place of rest.

SALESIAN MISSIONS

He Made and Loveth All

Speak, Lord,
for Thy servant heareth;
Speak peace to my anxious soul,
And help me to feel that all my ways
Are under Thy wise control;
That He who cares for the lily,
And heeds the sparrows' fall,
Shall tenderly lead His loving child:
For He made and loveth all.

UNKNOWN

The Spirit of Love

You will find, as you look back
upon your life, that the moments
when you have really lived are
the moments when you have
done things in the spirit of love.

HENRY DRUMMOND

Praise, Don't Complain

There is no mistaking, Lord. You've made it clear that I'm to be joyful in each and every task. The next time I'm tempted to complain about the mounds of work, remind me to turn the murmuring into praise. Amen.

Give Happiness

Whether any particular day shall
bring to you more of happiness or
of suffering is largely beyond your
power to determine. Whether each
day of your life shall give happiness
or suffering rests within yourself.

GEORGE S. MERRIAM

Every Task Matters

I long to accomplish great and noble
tasks, but it is my chief duty to
accomplish humble tasks as though
they were great and noble.
The world is moved along not only
by the mighty shoves of its heroes,
but also by the aggregate of the tiny
pushes of each honest worker.

HELEN KELLER

Confidence in God

I place no hope in my
strength, nor in my works:
but all my confidence is in
God my protector, who never
abandons those who have put all
their hope and thought in Him.

FRANÇOIS RABELAIS

Go Out in Joy

You will go out in joy and be led forth in peace; the mountains and hills will burst into song before you, and all the trees of the field will clap their hands.

ISAIAH 55:12 NIV

May Jesus Christ Be Praised!

When morning guilds the skies,
my heart awakening cries:
May Jesus Christ be praised! Alike
at work and prayer, to Jesus I repair:
May Jesus Christ be praised!

JOSEPH BARNBY

A Kind Father

God is a kind Father. He sets us all in the places where He wishes us to be employed; and that employment is truly "our Father's business." He chooses work for every creature. . . . He gives us always strength enough, and sense enough, for what He wants us to do.

JOHN RUSKIN

He Designed You

Your identity is the result of
neither coincidence nor
accident. You are who you are
because of God's loving design.
He wanted you to be *you*,
and no one else.

DARLENE SALA

The Light of Love, Faith, and Hope

In the dark dreary nights,
when the storm is at its most fierce,
the lighthouse burns bright so
the sailors can find their way home
again. In life the same light burns.
This light is fueled with love, faith,
and hope. And through life's most
fierce storms these three burn their
brightest so we also can find
our way home again.

UNKNOWN

Your Face Upturned

Bask in the sunshine of [God's] love.
Drink of the waters of His goodness.
Keep your face upturned to Him as
the flowers do to the sun. Look,
and your soul shall live and grow.

HANNAH WHITALL SMITH

Unchangeable Beauty

The beauty of the earth, the beauty of the sky, the order of the stars, the sun, the moon. . .their very loveliness is their confession of God: for who made these lovely mutable things, but He who is Himself unchangeable beauty?

AUGUSTINE

The Wonder of Living

The wonder of living is held
within the beauty of silence,
the glory of sunlight,
the sweetness of fresh spring air,
the quiet strength of earth,
and the love that lies at the
very root of all things.

UNKNOWN

Come Forth as Gold

We will all "come forth as gold"
if we understand that God is
sovereign and knows what is best,
even when we cannot understand
what is happening at the time.
He asks us to trust Him and to know
that He cares for us even when
we can't track Him.

SHIRLEY DOBSON

His Unfailing Love

*How priceless is your unfailing love!
Both high and low among men find
refuge in the shadow of your wings.
They feast on the abundance of your
house; you give them drink from your
river of delights. For with you is the
fountain of life; in your light
we see light.*

PSALM 36:7–9 NIV

Turn It into a Blessing

If anyone would tell you the shortest, surest way to happiness and all perfection, he must tell you to make it a rule to yourself to thank and praise God for everything that happens to you. For it is certain that whatever seeming calamity happens to you, if you thank and praise God for it, you turn it into a blessing.

UNKNOWN

From Miracle to Miracle

To be alive, to be able to see, to walk, to have a home. . . it's all a miracle. I have adopted the technique of living life from miracle to miracle.

ARTHUR RUBENSTEIN

Footprints on Your Soul

Life is full of people who will make you laugh, cry, smile until your face hurts, and so happy that you think you'll burst. But the ones who leave their footprints on your soul are the ones that keep your life going.

NATALIE BERNOT

Rejoice in Him

Father, praising You and rejoicing in You must be high on my priority list. Proclaiming Your love to others must never be lacking in my life. Thank You that I am able to rejoice in You! Amen.

Joy Without and Joy Within

To be a joy-bearer and a joy-giver says everything, for in our life, if one is joyful, it means that one is faithfully living for God, and that nothing else counts; and if one gives joy to others, one is doing God's work; with joy without and joy within, all is well.

JANET ERSKINE STUART

A New Song

He lifted me out of the slimy pit,
out of the mud and mire;
he set my feet on a rock and
gave me a firm place to stand.
He put a new song in my mouth,
a hymn of praise to our God.

PSALM 40:2–3 NIV

The Streams of Living Waters

See, the streams of living waters,
Springing from eternal love,
Well supply thy sons and daughters
And all fear of want remove:
Who can faint while such a river
Ever flows their thirst to assuage?
Grace which, like the Lord,
the Giver,
Never fails from age to age.

JOHN NEWTON

Thank You, Lord

Thank You, Lord, for Your love and faithfulness to us. Thank You for making us Your people, for allowing us to be the sheep of Your pasture. Thank You for allowing us to serve such a great God! Amen.

Believe

Faith is the root of all blessings.
Believe and you shall be saved;
believe and your needs must be
satisfied; believe and you cannot
but be comforted and happy.

JEREMY TAYLOR

Most Amazing Day

I thank You, God, for this most amazing day, for the leaping greenly spirits of trees, and for the blue dream of sky and for everything which is natural, which is infinite, which is yes.

E. E. CUMMINGS

The Focus of His Love

How blessed is God! And what a blessing he is! He's the Father of our Master, Jesus Christ, and takes us to the high places of blessing in him. Long before he laid down earth's foundations, he had us in mind had settled on us as the focus of his love.

EPHESIANS 1:3–4 MSG

An Angel's Song

Kind words are the music of the world. They have a power which seems to be beyond natural causes, as if they were some angel's song which had lost its way and come on earth.

FREDERICK WILLIAM FABER

Make the Lights Prevail

An optimist is a person who sees only the lights in the picture, whereas a pessimist sees only the shadows. An idealist, however, is one who sees the light and the shadows, but in addition sees something else: the possibility of changing the picture, of making the lights prevail over the shadows.

FELIX ADLER

No Cause of Fear

If the Lord be with us, we have no cause of fear. His eye is upon us, His arm over us, His ear open to our prayer—His grace sufficient, His promise unchangeable.

JOHN NEWTON

Pure and Lovely

The things we think on are the things
that feed our souls. If we think on
pure and lovely things, we shall grow
pure and lovely like them.

HANNAH WHITALL SMITH

Guide and Cheer Others

Our gifts and attainments are
not only to be light and warmth in
our own dwellings, but are also to
shine through the windows into
the dark night, to guide and cheer
bewildered travelers on the road.

HENRY WARD BEECHER

Get Some Distance

Every now and then go away,
have a little relaxation, for when
you come back to your work your
judgment will be surer. Go some
distance away because then the
work appears smaller and more
of it can be taken in at a glance.

LEONARDO DA VINCI

My Reward Awaits Me

Father, my daily problems come and go; yet if I remain steadfast and dedicated, doing the work You have given me to do, I am confident that my reward awaits me. Thank You, Lord. Amen.

Keep Thou Thy Dreams

Keep thou thy dreams—
The tissue of all wings
Is woven first of them;
From dreams are made
The precious and
imperishable things
Whose loveliness lives
on and does not fade.

VIRNA SHEARD

True Success

To appreciate beauty; to find the best in others; to give one's self; to leave the world a little better, whether by a healthy child, a garden patch, or a redeemed social condition; to have played and laughed with enthusiasm, and sung with exultation; to know even one life has breathed easier because you have lived. . .this is to have succeeded.

RALPH WALDO EMERSON

The Lord Is the Everlasting God

Why do you say. . ."My way is hidden from the LORD; my cause is disregarded by my God"? Do you not know? Have you not heard? The LORD is the everlasting God, the Creator of the ends of the earth. He will not grow tired or weary, and his understanding no one can fathom.

ISAIAH 40:27–28 NIV

Christ Dwells within Me

I know Christ dwells within me all the time, guiding me and inspiring me whenever I do or say anything—a light of which I caught no glimmer before it comes to me at the very moment when it is needed.

ST. THERESE OF LISIEUX

Our Hearts Are His

If we believe in Jesus, we've been
cast a lifeline. We've connected
ourselves to Him in faith,
and though we struggle to work out
our beliefs with consistency,
our hearts are truly His. That internal
confidence earned us the greatest
reward: eternity with our Savior.

PAMELA MCQUADE

Like Embroidery

Take your needle, my child,
and work at your pattern; it will
come out a rose by and by. Life is
like that; one stitch at a time taken
patiently, and the pattern will come
out all right, like embroidery.

OLIVER WENDELL HOLMES

His Infinity and Simplicity

God is infinite in His simplicity
and simple in His infinity.
Therefore He is everywhere and
is everywhere complete. He is
everywhere on account of His
infinity, and is everywhere
complete on account of His simplicity.

MEISTER ECKHART

Every Flower

The splendor of the rose and the whiteness of the lily do not rob the little violet of its scent nor the daisy of its simple charm. If every tiny flower wanted to be a rose, spring would lose its loveliness.

ST. THERESE OF LISIEUX

Look to This Day!

Look to this day! For it is life,
the very life of life. For yesterday
is but a dream, and tomorrow
is only a vision, but today well
lived makes every yesterday a
dream of happiness and
tomorrow a vision of hope.

KALIDASA

Rewards of the Simple Life

To find the universal elements enough; to find the air and the water exhilarating; to be refreshed by a morning walk or an evening saunter. . .to be thrilled by the stars at night; to be elated over a bird's nest or a wildflower in spring—these are some of the rewards of the simple life.

JOHN BURROUGHS

The World Is
Full of Beauty

There is beauty in the forest
When the trees are green and fair;
There is beauty in the meadow
When the wildflowers scent the air.
There is beauty in the sunlight
And the soft blue beams above.
Oh, the world is full of beauty
When the heart is full of love.

UNKNOWN

His Compassions Never Fail

This I call to mind and therefore I have hope: Because of the LORD's great love we are not consumed, for his compassions never fail. They are new every morning; great is your faithfulness.

LAMENTATIONS 3:21—23 NIV

His Everlasting Way

By following Jesus, you always head
in the right direction. Though the
way may seem dark or convoluted,
and you may often wonder if you're
on the right track, as His Spirit
leads you, you cannot go wrong.
Your powerful Lord directs you in
His everlasting way.

PAMELA MCQUADE

May Grace Leap Out at You

My prayer is that God will surprise you today. In your daily routine, in the stressful details of ordinary life, when you least expect it, may grace leap out at you, encouraging your heart.

ELLYN SANNA

Prayers Are Answered

Lord, when I see how You have
interceded on my behalf, I want
to fall on my face before You.
My prayers have been answered in
miraculous ways. In times when
all I could see was darkness, You
provided light and power and hope.
Amen.

Be Better

Always dream and shoot higher than you know how to. Don't bother just to be better than your contemporaries or predecessors. Try to be better than yourself.

WILLIAM FAULKNER

Follow Aspirations

Far away there in the sunshine
are my highest aspirations.
I may not reach them, but I can
look up and see their beauty,
Believe in them, and try
to follow where they lead.

LOUISA MAY ALCOTT

An Instrument of Thy Peace

Lord, make me an instrument of Thy peace. Where there is hatred, let me sow love. Where there is injury, pardon. Where there is doubt, faith. Where there is despair, hope. Where there is darkness, light. Where there is sadness, joy.

St. Francis of Assisi

Tremendous Treasure in Nature

If we are children of God, we have a tremendous treasure in nature and will realize that it is holy and sacred. We will see God reaching out to us in every wind that blows, every sunrise and sunset, every cloud in the sky, every flower that blooms, and every leaf that fades.

OSWALD CHAMBERS

DAY 173

My Strength and My Shield

The LORD is my strength and my shield; my heart trusts in him, and I am helped. My heart leaps for joy and I will give thanks to him in song.

PSALM 28:7 NIV

Peace at Last

May He support us all the day long,
till the shades lengthen, and the
evening comes, and the busy world is
hushed, and the fever of life is over,
and our work is done! Then in His
mercy may He give us a safe lodging
and a holy rest, and peace at last.

John Henry Cardinal Newman

In Your Peace

Calm me, O Lord,
as you stilled the storm,
Still me, O Lord,
keep me from harm.
Let all the tumult within me cease,
Enfold me, Lord, in Your peace.

CELTIC TRADITIONAL

Every Step

When we are facing dire troubles,
God never deserts us. As life ebbs
away, He does not step back from our
need. No, the Eternal One guides us
every step of the way, whether life is
joyous or discouraging. God never
gives up on you and never fails you.
So don't give up on yourself.

PAMELA MCQUADE

Brim Over

Oh! May the God of green hope fill you up with joy, fill you up with peace, so that your believing lives, filled with the life-giving energy of the Holy Spirit, will brim over with hope!

ROMANS 15:13 MSG

DAY 178

No Situation Too Chaotic

There is no situation so chaotic that
God cannot, from that situation,
create something that is surpassingly
good. He did it at the creation. He did
it at the cross. He is doing it today.

BISHOP MOULE

A Wilderness of Blossom

I know nothing so pleasant as to sit there on a summer afternoon, with the western sun flickering through the great elder-tree. . .where flowers and flowering shrubs are set as thick as grass in a field, a wilderness of blossom, interwoven, intertwined, wreathy, garland, profuse beyond all profusion.

MARY MITFORD

My Heart

My heart is like a singing bird
Whose nest is in a water'd shoot;
My heart is like an apple-tree
Whose boughs are bent
with thick-set fruit;
My heart is like a rainbow shell
That paddles in a halcyon sea;
My heart is gladder than all these,
Because my love is come to me.

CHRISTINA ROSSETTI

On the Right Path

Thank You for Your promise to preserve me if I love You, Father. I know that this is an eternal promise. What more incentive do I need to pursue a right walk with You? Keep me on the right path, Lord. Amen.

Become as Little Children

Take time for make-believe.
Abandon yourself in play. I think
God gives us an imagination for
a reason. Christ knows the
pressures we endure. Perhaps this
is one reason He encourages us
to "become as little children."

JEAN LUSH WITH PAM VREDEVELT

The Shepherd Guides

Left to our own agendas, we either run at breakneck speeds right past the pasture. . .or sit in the parched desert. The Shepherd. . .intervenes on our behalf to guide us. . .onto a quiet path and into a calmer faith.

PATSY CLAIRMONT

Life Is What We Are Alive To

Life is what we are alive to.
It is not length but breadth. . . .
Be alive to. . .goodness, kindness,
purity, love, history, poetry,
music, flowers, stars, God,
and eternal hope.

MALTBIE D. BABCOCK

God Has Promised

The same God who guides the
stars in their courses,
who directs the earth in its orbit,
who feeds the burning furnace
of the sun and keeps the stars
perpetually burning with their
fires—the same God has
promised to supply thy strength.

CHARLES H. SPURGEON

DAY 186

Never Lose an Opportunity

Never lose an opportunity of
seeing anything that is beautiful;
for beauty is God's handwriting—
a wayside sacrament. Welcome it
in every fair face, in every fair sky,
in every fair flower, and thank
God for it as a cup of blessing.

RALPH WALDO EMERSON

Opportunities of a Richer Service

It may be one more request than we think we can fulfill, one more responsibility that we think we can manage. . . . Interruptions never distracted Jesus. He accepted them as opportunities of a richer service.

RUTH BELL GRAHAM

His Promise Is Unchangeable

God can't break his word. And because his word cannot change, the promise is likewise unchangeable. We who have run for our very lives to God have every reason to grab the promised hope with both hands and never let go.

HEBREWS 6:18 MSG

A Friend Encourages

We occasionally have moments when we're perfectly content to feel gloomy. . . . Then along comes a friend who manages to encourage a smile, and if she tries really hard, can even send you into a fit of laughter.

ANITA WIEGAND

God's Grace

God's grace is too big, too great
to understand fully. So we must
take the moments of His grace
throughout the day with us:
the music of the songbird in
the morning, the kindness
shown in the afternoon,
and the restful sleep at night.

UNKNOWN

Faith Arms from Fear

No coward soul is mine,
No trembler in the world's
storm-troubled sphere:
I see heaven's glories shine,
And faith shines equal,
arming me from fear.

EMILY BRONTË

The Sweetest Things in Life

The best things in life are nearest:
breath in your nostrils, light in
your eyes, flowers at your feet,
duties at your hand, the path of
right just before you. Do not grasp
at the stars, but do life's plain
common work as it comes,
certain that daily duties and daily
bread are the sweetest things in life.

ROBERT LOUIS STEVENSON

Our Journey

In such a beautiful wilderness of wildflowers we are amused with the very variety and novelty of the scene so much that we in our pleasure lose all sense of weariness or fatigue in the length of our wandering and get to the end before we are aware of our journey.

JOHN CLARE

Through Faith in Christ Jesus

We must not sit still and look for miracles; up and doing, and the Lord will be with thee. Prayer and pains, through faith in Christ Jesus, will do anything.

GEORGE ELIOT

The Love of Christ

*I pray that out of his glorious riches
he may strengthen you with power
through his Spirit in your inner being,
so that Christ may dwell in your hearts
through faith. And I pray that you,
being rooted and established in love,
may have power. . .to grasp how wide
and long and high and deep is
the love of Christ.*

EPHESIANS 3:16–18 NIV

New-Created

And if tonight my soul may find
her peace in sleep, and sink in good
oblivion, and in the morning wake
like a new-opened flower, then
I have been dipped again in God,
and new-created.

D. H. LAWRENCE

He Calms

Father, I can't begin to count the number of times You've wrapped Your loving arms around me and calmed me in the midst of fears. You've drawn me near in times of sorrow and given me assurance when I've faced great disappointment. Amen.

All Your Heart Might Desire

May you always have walls for
the winds, a roof for the rain,
tea beside the fire, laughter to
cheer you, those you love near you,
and all your heart might desire.

IRISH BLESSING

Knowing That
She Hath Wings

Be like the bird that,
halting in its flight
Awhile on boughs too slight
Feels them give way beneath her,
and yet sings
Knowing that she hath wings.

VICTOR HUGO

All Delightful Conditions

Cherish your visions; cherish your
ideals; cherish the music that stirs in
your heart, the beauty that forms in
your mind, the loveliness that drapes
your purest thoughts, for out of them
will grow all delightful conditions,
all heavenly environment.

JAMES ALLEN

The Hand of God

Nothing touches my life that hasn't first passed through the hand of God. He knows what is best for me. I will trust His hand in my life, believing that He sees how all things work together.

UNKNOWN

Rest for Your Souls

"Come to me, all you who are weary and burdened, and I will give you rest. Take my yoke upon you and learn from me, for I am gentle and humble in heart, and you will find rest for your souls. For my yoke is easy and my burden is light."

MATTHEW 11:28–30 NIV

God Is Awake

Have courage for the great
sorrows of life and patience
for the small ones; and when you
have laboriously accomplished your
daily task, go to sleep in peace.
God is awake.

VICTOR HUGO

Continually Filled with Praise and Thanksgiving

Lord, I want my heart to continually be filled with praise and thanksgiving to You. Keep me anchored in the thought that all You do is for my good and glory. Only You are deserving of my praise and adoration. Amen.

Ideals Are Like Stars

Ideals are like stars; you will not succeed in touching them with your hands. But like the seafaring man on the desert of waters, you choose them as your guides, and following them you will reach your destiny.

CARL SCHURZ

Work for Your Hands

May there always be work for your hands to do, may your purse always hold a coin or two. May the sun always shine on your windowpane, may a rainbow be certain to follow each rain. May the hand of a friend always be near you, may God fill your heart with gladness to cheer you.

IRISH BLESSING

Put Love into Action

Love cannot remain by itself—
it has no meaning. Love has to be
put into action, and that action is
service. Whatever form we are,
able or disabled, rich or poor, it is
not how much we do, but how much
love we put in the doing; a lifelong
sharing of love with others.

MOTHER TERESA

Heaven Breaking Through

All that is sweet, delightful,
and amiable in this world, in the
serenity of the air, the fineness
of seasons, the joy of light,
the melody of sounds, the beauty
of colors, the fragrance of smells,
the splendor of precious stones,
is nothing else but heaven breaking
through the veil of this world.

WILLIAM LAW

He Supplies

*Now he who supplies seed
to the sower. . .will enlarge
the harvest of your righteousness
You will be made rich in every
way so that you can be generous
on every occasion.*

2 CORINTHIANS 9:10—11 NIV

I Shall Not Live in Vain

If I can stop one heart
from breaking,
I shall not live in vain;
If I can ease one life in the aching,
Or cool one pain,
Or help one fainting robin
Unto his nest again,
I shall not live in vain.

EMILY DICKINSON

In Every Human Being's Heart

Whether sixty or sixteen, there is in every human being's heart the lure of wonder, the unfailing childlike appetite of what's next, and the joy of the game of living.

SAMUEL ULLMAN

He Is Close Enough

We do not need to search for
heaven, over here or over there,
in order to find our eternal Father.
In fact, we do not even need to
speak out loud, for though we
speak in the smallest whisper or
the most fleeting thought,
He is close enough to hear us.

TERESA OF AVILA

My Hope

Lord, You are my hope in an often hopeless world. You are my hope of heaven, my hope of peace, my hope of change, purpose, and unconditional love. Fill the reservoir of my heart to overflowing with the joy that real hope brings. Amen.

Little Pockets of Happiness

Between the house and the
store there are little pockets of
happiness. A bird, a garden,
a friend's greeting, a child's smile,
a cat in the sunshine needing a
stroke. Recognize them or ignore
them. It's always up to you.

PAM BROWN

Look Around—See Christ

Look backward—
see Christ dying for you.
Look upward—
see Christ pleading for you.
Look inward—
see Christ living in you.
Look forward—
see Christ coming for you.

UNKNOWN

Abundant Life

Abundant life, full of good things on
this earth, spiritual peace and joy,
and full, satisfying relationships—
that's what God intends His people
to have. Because Jesus entered your
life, you've entered a new realm.
Life has taken on a new meaning,
because you know the Creator.

PAMELA MCQUADE

Meant to Be Immortal

Our Creator would never
have made such lovely days,
and have given us the deep
hearts to enjoy them, above and
beyond all thought, unless we
were meant to be immortal.

NATHANIEL HAWTHORNE

The Soul Is a Temple

The soul is a temple, and God is
silently building it by night and by
day. Precious thoughts are building
it, unselfish love is building it,
all-penetrating faith is building it.

HENRY WARD BEECHER

The Path of Peace

*Through the heartfelt mercies of our
God, God's Sunrise will break in upon
us, shining on those in the darkness,
those sitting in the shadow of death,
then showing us the way, one foot
at a time, down the path of peace.*

LUKE 1:78–79 MSG

It Is Well with My Soul

And Lord, haste the day
when my faith shall be sight,
The clouds be rolled back as a scroll;
The trump shall resound,
and the Lord shall descend,
Even so, it is well with my soul.

HORATIO G. SPAFFORD

God Knows

You do not know what you are going to do; the only thing you know is that God knows what He is doing. . . . It is this attitude that keeps you in perpetual wonder—you do not know what God is going to do next.

OSWALD CHAMBERS

A Cheerful Temper Joined with Innocence

A cheerful temper joined with innocence will make beauty attractive, knowledge delightful, and with good-natured. It will lighten sickness, poverty, and affliction; convert ignorance into amiable simplicity, and render deformity itself agreeable.

JOSEPH ADDISON

Press On

A new life begins for us with every second. Let us go forward joyously to meet it. We must press on, whether we will or no, and we shall walk better with our eyes before us than with them ever cast behind.

UNKNOWN

The Love of God Shine Forth from You

Let Jesus be in your heart,
Eternity in your spirit,
The world under your feet,
The will of God in your actions.
And let the love of God shine
forth from you.

CATHERINE OF GENOA

A Radiance of Thine

Help me to spread my fragrance
everywhere I go. Flood my
soul with Thy spirit and life.
Penetrate and possess my whole
being so utterly that all my life
may only be a radiance of Thine.

JOHN HENRY CARDINAL NEWMAN

Nothing to Worry About

Father, as long as I trust in Your presence, I have nothing to worry about. Nothing can separate me from You, because you are the strong protector, the mighty One who watches over me always.
I praise You, Lord, for Your protection. Amen.

Bathed in Sunlight

*If you are generous with the
hungry and start giving yourselves
to the down-and-out, your lives
will begin to glow in the darkness,
your shadowed lives will be
bathed in sunlight.*

ISAIAH 58:10 MSG

Wishes

I wish you sunshine on your path and storms to season your journey. I wish you peace—in the world in which you live and in the smallest corner of the heart where truth is kept. I wish you faith—to help define your living and your life. More I cannot wish you— except perhaps love—to make all the rest worthwhile.

ROBERT A. WARD

A Balance

The best and safest thing is
to keep a balance in your life,
acknowledge the great power
around us and in us. If you can
do that, and live that way, you are
really a wise man.

EURIPIDES

Don't Linger

Treasure your memories today—
but don't linger in the past,
mourning for the "good old days."
God's presence was with you each
moment of those days, and I know
He will fill your life with blessings—
but He is also with you today.
And he has a storehouse of blessing
He still waits to give you in the future.

ELLYN SANNA

Jesus

God will never, never, never let us down if we have faith and put our trust in Him. He will always look after us. So we must cleave to Jesus. Our whole life must simply be woven into Jesus.

MOTHER TERESA

His Hand

He hideth my soul in
the cleft of the rock
That shadows a dry, thirsty land;
He hideth my life with
the depths of His love,
And covers me there with His hand,
And covers me there with His hand.

FANNY CROSBY

Confidence

Such confidence as this is ours through Christ before God. Not that we are competent in ourselves to claim anything for ourselves, but our competence comes from God.

2 CORINTHIANS 3:4–5 NIV

What Love Looks Like

What does [love] look like?
It has hands to help others,
feet to hasten to the poor and needy,
eyes to see misery and want,
ears to hear the sighs and sorrows of
men. That is what love looks like.

ST. AUGUSTINE

His Constant Care

Father, I praise You for Your
support. When my strength fails,
Yours is always sufficient. Thank
You for Your constant love and care,
for picking out my cry and never
failing to rescue me. Amen.

You Can Give

How lovely to think that no one need wait a moment, we can start now, start slowly changing the world! How lovely that everyone, great and small, can make their contribution toward introducing justice straightaway. . . . And you can always, always give something, even if it is only kindness!

ANNE FRANK

Believe

When you come to the edge of all the light you have, and you must take a step into the darkness of the unknown, believe that one of two things will happen. Either there will be something solid for you to stand on—or you will be taught how to fly.

PATRICK OVERTON

We Thank the Keeper

For sunlit hours and visions clear,
For all remembered faces dear. . . .
For friends who shared the year's
long road,
And bore with us the
common load. . .
For insights won through
toils and tears,
We thank the Keeper of our years.

CLYDE MCGEE

Champions

Champions do not become champions when they win the event, but in the hours, weeks, months, and years they spend preparing for it. The victorious performance itself is merely the demonstration of their championship character.

T. ALAN ARMSTRONG

For God So Loved

*"For God so loved the world that
he gave his one and only Son,
that whoever believes in him shall
not perish but have eternal life.
For God did not send his Son into
the world to condemn the world,
but to save the world through him."*

JOHN 3:16–17 NIV

Another Day

The wonderful thing about
sunset, and much the same can
be said for sunrise, is that it
happens every day, and even if the
sunset itself is not spectacular,
it marks the beginning of
another day. It's a great time
to pause and take notice.

ELAINE ST. JAMES

Reflection

Reflection. . .enables our minds to
be stretched in three different
directions—the direction that leads
to a proper relationship with God,
the relationship that leads to a
healthy relationship with others,
and the relationship that leads to a
deeper understanding of oneself.

MARK CONNOLLY

Lift Them

We look at our burdens and heavy
loads and shrink from them; but as
we lift them and bind them with our
hearts, they become wings; and on
them we rise and soar toward God.

MRS. CHARLES E. COWMAN

Accomplishment

Look at a day when you are
supremely satisfied at the end.
It is not a day when you lounge
around doing nothing; it is when
you have had everything to do,
and you have done it.

MARGARET THATCHER

Your Strength

Because of Your strength, Lord, I can smile. When I need peace, You strengthen me on the inside. This is where I need You the most. Let me reflect Your strength so that others will be drawn to You, too. Amen.

Full Life

Life is full of beauty. Notice it.
Notice the bumblebee, the small
child, and the smiling faces.
Smell the rain, and feel the wind.
Live your life to the fullest potential,
and fight for your dreams.

ASHLEY SMITH

The Beautiful

A person should hear a little
music, read a little poetry,
and see a fine picture every day of
their life, in order that worldly cares
may not obliterate the sense of
the beautiful which God has
implanted in the human soul.

JOHANN WOLFGANG VON GOETHE

Attitude

Your living is determined not so
much by what life brings to you
as by the attitude you bring to life;
not so much by what happens to
you as by the way your mind
looks at what happens.

KAHLIL GIBRAN

Work Hard

Are you bored with life? Then throw yourself into some work you believe in with all your heart, live for it, die for it, and you will find happiness that you had thought could never be yours.

DALE CARNEGIE

With All Your Heart

Whatever you do, work at it with all your heart, as working for the Lord, not for men, since you know that you will receive an inheritance from the Lord as a reward. It is the Lord Christ you are serving.

COLOSSIANS 3:23–24 NIV

A Friend

So long as we love, we serve;
so long as we are loved by others,
I would say that we are indispensable;
and no man is useless while
he has a friend.

ROBERT LOUIS STEVENSON

Be Wholly Alive

Try as much as possible to be
wholly alive, with all your might,
and when you laugh, laugh like hell
and when you get angry, get good
and angry. Try to be alive. You will
be dead soon enough.

WILLIAM SAROYAN

A New Person

Father, thanks to You I get
to start over, fresh and clean,
because You have made me a
new person. I now have a
lifetime of new days to spend
any way I choose. Thank You for
Your never-ending forgiveness.
Amen.

Don't Wait

Don't wait until everything is just right. It will never be perfect. There will always be challenges, obstacles and less than perfect conditions. So what. Get started now. With each step you take, you will grow stronger and stronger, more and more skilled, more and more self-confident, and more and more successful.

MARK VICTOR HANSEN

Imagination

The most beautiful world is always entered through the imagination. If you wish to be something you are not—something fine, noble, good— you shut your eyes, and for one dreamy moment you are that which you long to be.

HELEN KELLER

DAY 256

Scripture

When you're looking for some sweetness in a sour life, turn to scripture. The scriptures are God's huge love letter to His own people. As even the newest believer reads attentively, God's mercy becomes clear. Yet a lifelong believer can read the same passage and see something new again and again.

PAMELA MCQUADE

Encourage and Love

Flatter me, and I may not believe you. Criticize me, and I may not like you. Ignore me, and I may not forgive you. Encourage me, and I will not forget you. Love me, and I may be forced to love you.

WILLIAM ARTHUR WARD

Heaven

Lord, I know there will come a day
when we will be in heaven with You.
I look forward to that time, and I
thank You for the opportunity to
share that time and place with You.
Amen.

An Offering

*Take your everyday, ordinary
life—your sleeping, eating,
going-to-work, and walking-around
life—and place it before God as
an offering. Embracing what
God does for you is the best thing
you can do for him.*

ROMANS 12:1 MSG

Believe You Can

Men often become what they
believe themselves to be. If I believe
I cannot do something, it makes
me incapable of doing it. But when
I believe I can, then I acquire the
ability to do it even if I didn't
have it in the beginning.

MAHATMA GANDHI

Getting Started

The secret of getting ahead is getting started. The secret of getting started is breaking your complex overwhelming tasks into small manageable tasks, and then starting on the first one.

MARK TWAIN

Love

Love is friendship that has caught
fire. It is quiet understanding,
mutual confidence, sharing and
forgiving. It is loyalty through good
and bad times. It settles for less
than perfection and makes
allowances for human weaknesses.

ANN LANDERS

To God All Praise and Glory!

What God's almighty power hath made
His gracious mercy keepeth,
By morning glow or evening shade
His watchful eye ne'er sleepeth.
Within the kingdom of His might,
Lo! All is just and all is right:
To God all praise and glory!

JOHANN J. SCHÜTZ

DAY 264

And Give You Peace

*"The Lord bless you and keep you;
the Lord make his face shine
upon you and be gracious to you;
the Lord turn his face toward you
and give you peace."*

NUMBERS 6:24–26 NIV

Open Wide

Open wide the windows of our spirits and fill us full of light; open wide the door of our hearts that we may receive and entertain Thee with all the powers of our adoration.

CHRISTINA ROSSETTI

A Gentle Word

A gentle word, like summer rain,
may soothe some heart
and banish pain.
What joy or sadness often springs
from just the simple little things!

WILLA HOEY

Climb Higher

Why should we live halfway up the hill and swathed in the mists, when we might have an unclouded sky with a radiant sun over our heads if we would climb higher and walk in the light of His face?

ALEXANDER MACLAREN

No Despair

One of the best safeguards of our hopes. . .is to be able to mark off the areas of hopelessness and to acknowledge them, to face them directly, not with despair but with the creative intent of keeping them from polluting all the areas of possibility.

William F. Lynch

Those Who Love

Those who love are borne on wings; they run and are filled with joy; they are free and unrestricted. . . . Beyond all things they rest in the one highest thing, from whom streams all that is good.

THOMAS À KEMPIS

I Wish

When you are lonely, I wish you love;
When you are down, I wish you joy;
When you are troubled,
I wish you peace. . .
When things are chaotic,
I wish you inner silence;
At all times I wish you
the God of hope.

UNKNOWN

By Grace

*For it is by grace you have been saved,
through faith—and this not from
yourselves, it is the gift of God—not by
works, so that no one can boast. For
we are God's workmanship, created in
Christ Jesus to do good works, which
God prepared in advance for us to do.*

EPHESIANS 2:8–10 NIV

Wonderful Life

Coming to Jesus brings us new life.
Not just a few more years on earth
or a better way of living, but real,
exciting, wonderful life. Existence
free from the necessity of constant
sin. The ability to do right things for
the right reasons. Life connected
to God Himself.

PAMELA MCQUADE

Obedience

All of God's revealed truths
are sealed until they are
opened to us through
obedience. Even the smallest
bit of obedience opens heaven.

OSWALD CHAMBERS

A Wonderful Name

Jesus. What a wonderful name!
It is the only name we need to call
upon for salvation. I praise You for
being the Way, the Truth, and the
Life, Lord. Amen.

Christian Faith

Christian faith is like a grand cathedral, with divinely pictured windows. Standing without, you can see no glory, nor can imagine any. But standing within, every ray of light reveals a harmony of unspeakable splendors.

NATHANIEL HAWTHORNE

DAY 276

God Knows

God knows everything about us.
And He cares about everything.
Moreover, He can manage every
situation. And He loves us! Surely
this is enough to open the
wellsprings of joy. . . . And joy is
always a source of strength.

HANNAH WHITALL SMITH

By the Grace of God

I am not what I ought to be; I am not what I wish to be; I am not what I hope to be, but, by the grace of God, I am not what I was.

JOHN NEWTON

Our Dwelling Place

When we are told that God, who is our
dwelling place, is also our fortress,
it can only mean one thing. . .that if
we will but live in our dwelling place,
we shall be perfectly safe and secure.

HANNAH WHITALL SMITH

Laughter

Sense of humor, God's great gift,
causes spirits to uplift;
Helps to make our bodies mend,
lightens burdens, cheers a friend;
Tickles children, elders grin at this
warmth that glows within;
Surely in the great hereafter,
heaven must be full of laughter!

UNKNOWN

All Prepared

*Like an open book, you watched me grow
from conception to birth; all the stages
of my life were spread out before you,
the days of my life all prepared before
I'd even lived one day.*

PSALM 139:16 MSG

Welcoming

Lord, You welcomed me into
Your family with love and
acceptance. Help me be as kind
to others as You have been
to me—cheerfully welcoming
everyone. Amen.

God Is Great

I belong to the "Great God Party"
and will have nothing to do with the
"Little God Party." Christ does not
want nibblers of the possible,
but grabbers of the impossible.

C. T. STUDD

Unending Praise

May your life become one of glad
and unending praise to the Lord
as you journey through this world,
and in the world that is to come!

TERESA OF AVILA

Come, Thou Fount

Come, Thou Fount of every blessing,
tune my heart to sing Thy grace;
Streams of mercy, never ceasing,
call for songs of loudest praise.
Teach me some melodious sonnet,
sung by flaming tongues above;
Praise the mount—I'm fixed upon it—
mount of Thy redeeming love.

ROBERT ROBINSON

His Ability Is Great

If you have a special need today, focus your full attention on the goodness and greatness of your Father rather than on the size of your need. Your need is so small compared to His ability to meet it.

More

More faith in my Savior,
more sense of His care;
More joy in His service,
more purpose in prayer. . .
More fit for the kingdom,
more used would I be;
More blessed and holy,
more, Savior, like Thee.

PHILIP P. BLISS

Faith and Love

Faith, like light, should always be simple and unbending; while love, like warmth, should beam forth on every side and bend to every necessity of our brethren.

MARTIN LUTHER

Pressing On

*Forgetting what is behind and
straining toward what is ahead,
I press on toward the goal to win the
prize for which God has called me
heavenward in Christ Jesus.*

PHILIPPIANS 3:13–14 NIV

He Guides

Father, thank You for Your promise to guide me in all things great and small. Your eye is always on me, keeping me from error and ensuring that I can always find a way home to You. Amen.

The Glory of Friendship

The glory of friendship is. . .the
spiritual inspiration that comes
to one when he discovers that
someone else believes in him
and is willing to trust him
with his friendship.

RALPH WALDO EMERSON

DAY 291

Rest, Don't Quit!

When things go wrong,
as they sometimes will,
When the road you're
trudging seems all uphill. . .
When care is pressing
you down a bit,
Rest, if you must—
but don't you quit!

UNKNOWN

If Only You Ask

Facing a tough time? See it as a chance to learn just how faithful your Lord is. Then thank Him that though you can't rejoice that you face the circumstances, you can be glad He's by your side every step of the way. He will be there for you— if only you ask.

PAMELA MCQUADE

Step Out

Let us step into the darkness
and reach out for the hand
of God. The path of faith and
darkness is so much safer
than the one we would
choose by sight.

GEORGE MACDONALD

DAY 294

Do Not Fear

So do not fear, for I am with you;
do not be dismayed, for I am your God.
I will strengthen you and help you;
I will uphold you with my righteous
right hand.

ISAIAH 41:10 NIV

Today

Today Jesus is working just as
wonderful works as when He
created the heaven and the earth.
His wondrous grace,
His wonderful omnipotence,
is for His child who needs Him
and who trusts Him, even today.

CHARLES E. HURLBURT AND T. C. HORTON

Look It in the Eye

If I were asked to give what I consider the single most useful bit of advice for all humanity it would be this: Expect trouble as an inevitable part of life and when it comes, hold your head high, look it squarely in eye, and say, "I will be bigger than you. You cannot defeat me."

Ann Landers

Content through Praise

The thought of You stirs us so deeply that we cannot be content unless we praise You, because You have made us for Yourself and our hearts find no peace until they rest in You.

ST. AUGUSTINE

Take Hold

Take hold of this good gift God has
for you. Accept the bad news that
you've sinned, and offer that wrong
up to Him. He'll reply with the Good
News that Jesus died for it all,
and your repentance has already
given you the best His kingdom has to
offer: forgiveness for every sin.

PAMELA MCQUADE

Blessed Assurance

Blessed assurance,
Jesus is mine!
Oh, what a foretaste
of glory divine!
Heir of salvation,
purchase of God,
Born of His Spirit,
washed in His blood.

FANNY J. CROSBY

Jesus Is Light

I heard the voice of Jesus say:
"I am this dark world's light;
Look unto Me, thy morn shall rise,
and all thy day be bright."
I looked to Jesus, and I found
in Him my Star, my Sun;
And in that light of life,
I'll walk till traveling days are done!

HORATIUS BONAR

His Great Love

*Because of his great love for us,
God, who is rich in mercy,
made us alive with Christ
even when we were dead in
transgressions—it is by
grace you have been saved.*

EPHESIANS 2:4–5 NIV

Nothing Compares

Nothing can compare to the beauty
and greatness of the soul in which
our King dwells in His full majesty.
No earthly fire can compare with the
light of its blazing love. No bastions
can compare with its ability
to endure forever.

TERESA OF AVILA

Count Your Blessings

Count your blessings;
name them one by one.
Count your blessings;
see what God has done!
Count your blessings;
name them one by one.
Count your many blessings;
see what God has done!

JOHNSON OATMAN JR.

Friends Help

My friends have made the story of my life. In a thousand ways they have turned my limitations into beautiful privileges and enabled me to walk serene and happy in the shadow cast by my deprivation.

HELEN KELLER

Through Every Storm

We shall steer safely through every storm, so long as our heart is right, our intention fervent, our courage steadfast, and our trust fixed on God.

St. Francis de Sales

He Delivers

Lord, I do not know how to deliver
myself from temptation, but You
know the way. You have been there.
When I stumble, I know Your arms
will catch me; if I fall, You bring me
to my feet and guide me onward.
Amen.

Blessing on Blessing

God, who is love—who is, if I
may say it this way, made out
of love—simply cannot help but
shed blessing on blessing upon us.
We do not need to beg, for He
simply cannot help it!

HANNAH WHITALL SMITH

Loving the Lord

My love of You, O Lord, is not some vague feeling: It is positive and certain. Your Word struck into my heart and from that moment I loved You. Besides this, all about me, heaven and earth and all that they contain proclaim that I should love You.

ST. AUGUSTINE

Not All

This life is not all. It is an
"unfinished symphony"...with
those who know that they are
related to God and have felt
"the power of an endless life."

HENRY WARD BEECHER

Take Heart

"I have told you these things, so that in me you may have peace. In this world you will have trouble. But take heart! I have overcome the world."

JOHN 16:33 NIV

Through Hard Times

It's usually through our hard times, the unexpected and not-according-to-plan times, that we experience God in more intimate ways. We discover an unquenchable longing to know Him more.

UNKNOWN

Fear vs. Faith

Fear imprisons, faith liberates;
fear paralyzes, faith empowers;
fear disheartens, faith encourages;
fear sickens, faith heals; fear makes
useless, faith makes serviceable—
and most of all, fear puts hopelessness
at the heart of life, while faith
rejoices in its God.

HARRY EMERSON FOSDICK

An Infinite God

An infinite God can give all of
Himself to each of His children.
He does not distribute Himself
that each may have a part, but to
each one He gives all of Himself
as fully as if there were no others.

A. W. TOZER

Working Faith

This is a sane, wholesome, practical working faith: That it is man's business to do the will of God; second, that God Himself takes on the care of that man; and third, that therefore that man ought never to be afraid of anything.

GEORGE MACDONALD

All That We See

God has not made a little universe.
He has made the wide stretches
of space and has put there all the
flaming hosts we see at night, all the
planets, stars, and galaxies.
Wherever we go, let us remind
ourselves that God has made
everything we see. . . . And not only
did God make it all, but He is present.

FRANCIS A. SCHAEFFER

The God of Love and Peace

May the God of love and peace set your heart at rest and speed you on your journey. May He meanwhile shelter you. . .in the place of complete plenitude where you will repose forever in the vision of peace, in the security of trust, and in the restful enjoyment of His riches.

RAYMOND OF PENYAFORT

A Different Sort of Evidence

Faith does not mean believing without evidence. It means believing in realities that go beyond sense and sight—for which a totally different sort of evidence is required.

JOHN BAILLIE

The Inner Fire

In everyone's life, at some time,
our inner fire goes out. It is then
burst into flame by an encounter
with another human being.
We should all be thankful for those
people who rekindle the inner spirit.

ALBERT SCHWEITZER

His Name Proclaimed

"I have raised you up for this very
purpose, that I might show you my
power and that my name might be
proclaimed in all the earth."

EXODUS 9:16 NIV

Renew Me

As I learn to rest in You, Lord,
renew me. Give me the ability I
need to be patient, no matter
what trouble is around me. Let my
joyful hope and faithful prayers
build up my patience. Amen.

DAY 321

God Seeks You

If you are seeking after God,
you may be sure of this:
God is seeking you much more.
He is the Lover, and you are
His beloved. He has promised
Himself to you.

JOHN OF THE CROSS

Promises Kept

We may. . .depend upon God's
promises, for. . .he will be as good
as His word. He is so kind that He
cannot deceive us, so true that He
cannot break His promise.

MATTHEW HENRY

So Small a Thing

Is it so small a thing to have
enjoyed the sun, to have lived
light in the spring, to have loved,
to have thought, to have done;
to have advanced true friends?

MATTHEW ARNOLD

Limitless Hope

When we take time to notice the simple things in life, we never lack for encouragement. We discover we are surrounded by limitless hope that's just wearing everyday clothes.

UNKNOWN

His Divine Power

*His divine power has given us
everything we need for life and
godliness through our knowledge
of him who called us by his
own glory and goodness.*

2 PETER 1:3 NIV

Love Is the Key

Love is the key. Joy is love singing.
Peace is love resting. Long-suffering is
love enduring. Kindness is love's touch.
Goodness is love's character.
Faithfulness is love's habit.
Gentleness is love's self-forgetfulness.
Self-control is love holding the reins.

DONALD GREY BARNHOUSE

Grace

We know certainly that our God. . .
gives us every grace, every abundant
grace; and though we are so weak of
ourselves, this grace is able to carry us
through every obstacle and difficulty.

ELIZABETH ANN SETON

As Flowers

As flowers carry dewdrops,
trembling on the edges of the
petals and ready to fall at the first
waft of the wind or brush of bird,
so the heart should carry its beaded
words of thanksgiving. At the first
breath of heavenly flavor, let down
the shower, perfumed with the
heart's gratitude.

HENRY WARD BEECHER

A Thankful Spirit

First among the things to be
thankful for is a thankful spirit. . . .
Happy are they who possess
this gift! Blessings may fail and
fortunes vary, but the thankful
heart remains.

UNKNOWN

Thanksgiving

*Enter his gates with thanksgiving
and his courts with praise; give
thanks to him and praise his name.
For the LORD is good and his love
endures forever; his faithfulness
continues through all generations.*

PSALM 100:4–5 NIV

A Loving Thought

If instead of a gem, or even a flower, we should cast the gift of a loving thought into the heart of a friend, that would be giving as the angels give.

GEORGE MACDONALD

He Answers

Do you long for help from God?
Your desire is in the right place.
Just ask, then trust He will answer.
Tomorrow may not solve every
problem, but you can know that help
is on the way. You've put your faith
in the eternal God who never fails.
Talk to Him this morning,
and watch help appear.

PAMELA McQUADE

Hope Thou

Knowest thou not that day
follows night, that flood comes
after ebb, that spring and
summer succeed winter?
Hope thou then! Hope thou ever!
God fails thee not.

CHARLES H. SPURGEON

May the Sun Always Shine

May the sun always shine on your windowpane; may a rainbow be certain to follow each rain; may the hand of a friend always be near you; may God fill your heart with gladness to cheer you.

IRISH BLESSING

Immeasurable Love

We are so preciously loved by God
that we cannot comprehend it.
No created being can ever know how
much and how sweetly and tenderly
God loves them. It is only with the
help of His grace that we are able to
persevere in spiritual contemplation
with endless wonder at His high,
surpassing, immeasurable love which
our Lord in His goodness has for us.

JULIAN OF NORWICH

How Can I Keep from Singing?

My life flows on in endless song;
Above earth's lamentation
I hear the sweet though
far-off hymn
That hails a new creation. . . .
Since God is Lord of
heaven and earth,
How can I keep from singing?

UNKNOWN

Not Alone

Lord, direct me daily to accept and apply the strength that You've offered, so that I will truly have the gentle spirit that You intend me to have. Thank You, Jesus, that I don't have to do this on my own. Amen.

Promise of a Better Day

From far beyond our world of
trouble and care and change,
our Lord shines with undimmed
light, a radiant, guiding Star to all
who will follow Him—a morning
Star, promise of a better day.

CHARLES E. HURLBURT AND T. C. HORTON

Surprises

In all our lives, in many simple,
familiar, homely ways, God infuses
this element of joy from the
surprises of life, which unexpectedly
brighten our days, and fill
our eyes with light.

HENRY WADSWORTH LONGFELLOW

Wonderful Things

God has wonderful things in mind
for you. If you ask, He'll show you
what gifts He's given you and how
He wants you to bless others with
them. Don't wait until eternity to
experience the joys and delights
of faith—share some of that good
news today!

PAMELA MCQUADE

Jesus

The word which became flesh
has a name. And approaching
this day of days, at this season
of seasons, let the splendor of
that Man above men sparkle
upon your lips. Jesus.

JAMES SMETHAM

Just Be

Don't get so busy that you forget to simply *be*. Sometimes the best way to stop being overwhelmed by life is to simply step back, take a day. . . or an hour. . .or a moment, and notice all that God is doing in your life.

ELLYN SANNA

Day 343

The Son of the Most High

"You will be with child and give birth to a son, and you are to give him the name Jesus. He will be great and will be called the Son of the Most High. The Lord God will give him the throne of his father David, and. . . his kingdom will never end."

Luke 1:31–33 niv

From Faith to Faith

Trust in your Redeemer's strength. . .
exercise what faith you have, and by
and by He shall rise upon you with
healing beneath His wings. Go from
faith to faith and you shall receive
blessing upon blessing.

CHARLES H. SPURGEON

Without Fear

We walk without fear,
full of hope and courage and
strength to do His will, waiting
for the endless good which He
is always giving as fast as He
can get us able to take it in.

GEORGE MACDONALD

His Touch

The Lord's chief desire is to reveal
Himself to you and, in order
for Him to do that, He gives you
abundant grace. The Lord gives you
the experience of enjoying His
presence. He touches you, and His
touch is so delightful that, more than
ever, you are drawn inwardly
to Him.

MADAME JEANNE GUYON

He Will Provide

Each of us may be sure that if
God sends us on stony paths He
will provide us with strong shoes,
and He will not send us out on
any journey for which He does
not equip us well.

ALEXANDER MACLAREN

A Savior Born

*"Do not be afraid. I bring you good
news of great joy that will be for all
the people. Today in the town of David
a Savior has been born to you;
he is Christ the Lord."*

LUKE 2:10—11 NIV

God Came to Us

God came to us because God
wanted to join us on the road,
to listen to our story, and to help
us realize that we are not walking
in circles but moving toward the
house of peace and joy.

THOMAS MERTON

In His Hands

Heavenly Father, I long for Your peace in my heart. Please take every anxious thread, every tightly pulled knot of uncertainty, sorrow, conflict, and disappointment into Your gentle, loving hands. Amen.

A Garden

To know someone here or there with whom you feel there is an understanding in spite of distances or thoughts unexpressed—that can make of this earth a garden.

JOHANN WOLFGANG VON GOETHE

Eternity

Eternity is the divine treasure house, and hope is the window, by means of which mortals are permitted to see, as through a glass darkly, the things which God is preparing.

WILLIAM MOUNTFORD

Happiness

Happiness is a sunbeam. . . .
When it strikes a kindred heart,
like the converged lights upon
a mirror, it reflects itself with
redoubled brightness. It is not
perfected until it is shared.

JANE PORTER

That It Should Take Place in Me

We are celebrating the feast of the Eternal Birth which God the Father has borne and never ceases to bear in all eternity. . . . But if it takes not place in me, what avails it? Everything lies in this, that it should take place in me.

MEISTER ECKHART

Humble Yourself

"If my people, who are called by my name, will humble themselves and pray and seek my face and turn from their wicked ways, then will I hear from heaven and will forgive their sin and will heal their land."

2 CHRONICLES 7:14 NIV

His Mystery, Your Promise

Trust God where you cannot trace Him. Do not try to penetrate the clouds He brings over you; rather look to the bow that is on it. The mystery is God's; the promise is yours.

JOHN R. MACDUFF

Born to Deliver

Born Thy people to deliver,
Born a child and yet a king.
Born to reign in us forever,
Now Thy gracious kingdom bring.
By Thine own eternal Spirit
Rule in all our hearts alone;
By Thine all sufficient merit,
Raise us to Thy glorious throne.

CHARLES WESLEY

When Christ Was Born

A thrill of hope the
weary world rejoices,
For yonder breaks a
new and glorious morn.
Fall on your knees,
O, hear the angel voices.
O night divine, O night
when Christ was born!

JOHN S. DWIGHT

Prince of Wholeness

*For a child has been born—for us!
the gift of a son—for us! He'll take
over the running of the world.
His names will be: Amazing Counselor,
Strong God, Eternal Father, Prince
of Wholeness. His ruling authority
will grow, and there'll be no limits
to the wholeness he brings.*

ISAIAH 9:6–7 MSG

Heaven for Us All

Many merry Christmases,
many happy New Years.
Unbroken friendships,
great accumulations of
cheerful recollections
and affections on earth,
and heaven for us all.

CHARLES DICKENS

The Spirit of Love

You will find as you look back
upon your life that the moments
when you have truly lived are the
moments when you have done
things in the spirit of love.

HENRY DRUMMOND

Creator of Light

O God, creator of light: at the rising of Your sun this morning, let the greatest of all lights, Your love, rise like the sun within our hearts.

Armenian Apostolic Church

What God Will Do

You never can measure what God will do through you. . . . Keep your relationship right with Him, then whatever circumstances you are in, and whoever you meet day by day, He is pouring rivers of living water through you.

OSWALD CHAMBERS

In God's Heart

A room of quiet—
a temple of peace;
A home of faith—
where doubtings cease;
A house of comfort—
where hope is given;
A source of strength—
to make earth heaven;
A shrine of worship—
a place to pray—
I found all this—
in God's heart today.

UNKNOWN

Never-Ending Blessings

Heavenly Father, I have so much to be thankful for. My list of blessings is never-ending. May I never fail to praise You and to thank You for the many blessings You have given to me. Amen.

Scripture Index

Old Testament

New Testament

Notes

Notes

_____

_____

_____

_____

_____

_____

_____

_____

Notes

Notes

Notes

Notes